Boom Boom!

Boomwhackers® on Broadway

- **Cool CD With Full Performance and Accompaniment Tracks**
- **Teaching Suggestions and Reproducible Visuals**
- **10 Great Broadway Tunes**

This is a joint publication between Warner Bros. Publications and Whacky Music, Inc.

BOOMWHACKERS® Tuned Percussion Tubes are a product of Whacky Music, Inc., of Sedona, Arizona.

"BOOMWHACKERS" is a registered trademark licensed to Whacky Music, Inc. Visit the Whacky Music Web site at www.boomwhackers.com.

Arranger/Editor: Gayle Giese
Consultant: Chris Judah-Lauder
Recording Producer: Teena Chinn
Art Cover Design: Nancy Rehm
Music Engraving and Text Layout: Adrian Alvarez
Text Editor: Nadine DeMarco
Production Coordinator: Sheryl Rose

General Teaching Suggestions

Although teaching suggestions are provided for each song, here are some general tips to help you and your students thoroughly enjoy playing the ten fun Broadway songs in this book.

Use the cool CD that is included! Before teaching the Boomwhacker® parts for a particular song, play the full performance version on the CD so that students will get the song in their ears. After students are familiar with the song, assign parts and distribute the Boomwhackers®.

Reproducible teaching visuals are also provided. The musical notes used on the visuals have open noteheads so that you can color them in with colors that match the Boomwhacker® tubes. These visuals may be photocopied and placed on music stands for the students. You could ask students to color in the noteheads they will play as a learning experience; for example, ask them to find all the C notes and color them red. You might prefer to copy the visuals onto transparencies and use them as overheads, coloring in the noteheads with overhead markers.

Once students have the skills to play through the entire song, they will enjoy playing and performing with the accompaniment tracks on the CD. Occasionally, you'll hear some melody notes even on the accompaniment tracks to reinforce the tune when the Boomwhacker® melody part may be difficult for some players. Of course, students may also play along with the full performance tracks. Clicks sound at the start of each track to set the tempo and allow students to prepare to play.

Occasionally, tremolos or rolls or even repeated pitches appear because the tubes make a staccato rather than a sustaining sound. Practice the tremolos (some teachers may prefer to call these "rolls") by having students hold an empty hand close to the floor, thigh, or other playing surface and quickly bounce the tube back and forth between the surface and the hand (fingers or palm). Another way is to sit on the floor with feet about five inches apart and bounce the tube back and forth between the shoe soles. Sneakers work great! If the student is standing with feet shoulder-width apart, the tubes can be bounced between knees. Experiment!

Octavator™ caps are available for Boomwhacker® tubes, and they are super! These caps easily attach to either end of the tube and lower the tube's pitch by an octave, creating a very resonant sound. When using the caps, students can hold the tube perpendicular to the floor and gently bounce the capped end of the tube on the floor. The sound is best on a lightly carpeted surface; strips of felt can be placed on a hard surface. Use the caps or the bass tubes whenever you see *8vb* below the notes in arrangements within this book. (In the "Required Tubes" section, these are listed as "Low" pitches.) Many arrangements suggest *8vb* throughout the accompaniment part so that it sounds in the range of most left-hand piano parts.

All ten songs in this book require the use of at least one set of the eight C Major Diatonic Scale tubes and one set of the Bass Diatonic set of seven tubes. Another option (preferred by th editor) is to use two C Major Diatonic sets and place Octavator™ caps on one set. Additional sets provide more teaching flexibility, allowing students to hold a tube in each hand or to have several students play tubes of the same pitch. For some songs, you may want to strengthen the melody by having more melody players than accompaniment players. Of the ten Broadway songs in this book, three songs have very limited optional uses for chromatic tubes. However, "If I Were a Rich Man" requires the use of chromatic tubes if you want Boomwhackers® to play the melody part; chromatic tubes are not needed if you want your students to play just the accompaniment patterns with the melody on the CD, piano, or other instrument such as violin or clarinet. "Let the Sunshine In" requires G♯ and F♯ tubes in the accompaniment part. The use of chromatic and diatonic tubes is indicated in the "Required Tubes" section for each song.

Chord symbols have been added in this book in case you would like to accompany your students on piano or guitar or reference the harmonic changes for teaching purposes.

Arrangements were written for upper elementary and middle school general music classes, offering both melody and accompaniment parts. You may teach all parts or only one part or section and play it along with the CD. Feel free to adapt the arrangements depending on the skill and number of students in your classes. All parts in the visuals and the score are shown in treble clef.

Finally, have fun! These are familiar songs that students will be eager to play—and now they can play them on the fun Boomwhacker® musical tubes.

—the Editor

Contents

Editor's Note

This songbook is one of a series of materials for Boomwhackers® Musical Tubes being jointly developed by Warner Bros. Publications and Whacky Music, Inc., which manufactures Boomwhackers®. Whacky Music recognizes the important value these materials add to its unique musical tubes and is proud to have the opportunity to cooperate with Warner Bros. Publications in their development.

The color-coded, plastic Boomwhackers® tubes were invented by Craig Ramsell, president of Whacky Music, after being inspired by a cardboard gift-wrap tube that he had cut in two in preparation for recycling. As of this writing in 2002, more than one million Boomwhackers® have been shipped into the world. Because they are fun, easy to play, and inexpensive, a large number of them are being used in thousands of schools around the world for music education. They have received numerous awards, including a Parents' Choice Gold Award, Dr. Toy's Best 100 Children's Products, and an Oppenheim Toy Portfolio Gold Seal.

I Don't Need Anything but You

Tubes required:

(Tubes are listed in order of occurrence in the music for each part. For the "Low" tubes, use bass tubes or tubes with Octavator™ caps. Suggested tube distribution appears in the teaching suggestions below.)
This piece may be played with only three diatonic sets with Octavator™ caps, without doubling any parts. Four sets are recommended.

Introduction: E, G   F, A   C, E   (opt.: Low B), D

Melody: It is suggested that the melody be used from the CD or played on a keyboard instrument.

Accompaniment: Low G   Low A   Low E   Low D   Low C   Low F   Low B
       F   D   G   E   C   A
Optional: Very Low C (two octaves below C: use a bass tube with an Octavator™ cap).

Teaching suggestions:

IDENTIFYING METER CHANGES
- Using the Boomwhackers® Visual, have students find the tempo changes to 3/4 and back to 4/4. Listen to the CD and patsch the steady beat (four beats per measure in 4/4 and three beats per measure in 3/4). Repeat, clapping the three beats in 3/4 time and patsching the four beats in 4/4 time.

INTRODUCTION (and final four measures)
- Each student should have two tubes of different pitches, one in each hand. Seat these children together:
   - One student holds G and A
   - One student holds E and F
   - One student holds C and E
   - One student holds D and (opt.) Low B
- Tell the entire class to listen to the introduction on the CD and then look at the Boomwhackers® Visual (see page 8) and practice patsching the rhythms before playing them. Have the entire class patsch all four measures; then have just the intro players patsch their own parts in rhythm (patsching only their notes) before they play their tubes. The G, A and E, F players repeat their parts four measures from the end. Color-code the visual notes to match the tubes, if needed.
- The last four measures are like the introduction except for the final measure, which anyone holding a C tube may play.

ACCOMPANIMENT
- Echoed phrases (measures 5–12 and measures 20–27)
   - Distribute tubes:
      - One student holds Low G and Low A
      - One student holds Low E and Low D
   - Seat the two groups next to each other.

Listen to the CD where the melody begins (measure 5). Next, sing and have all students echo you, singing in rhythm:

> Together at last, (students echo)
> Together forever. (students echo "ever")
> We're tying a knot (students echo)
> They never can sever. (students echo "sever")

Repeat with students patsching the echoed rhythm. See how these rhythms are notated on the Boomwhackers® Visual; color-code the notes if it's helpful to your class. Once the rhythms are solid, have just the Low G and Low A and Low E and Low D players practice playing the patterns on their tubes.

• **Measures 13–18 and 28–32**

Distribute tubes for measures 13–18 and 28–32:

> One student holds Low C and Low F
> Low D, Low E, and Low G have already been assigned (see above)

Use the visual and color-code the notes. Watch for rests in measures 17–18.

• **Soli measures 19–20**

Distribute tubes. Students playing this part should hold pitches that are next to each other:

> One student holds Low C and Low G
> One student holds Low A and Low B

Find the Boomwhackers® soli part in measure 19. Listen to it on the CD and look at it on the visual. Practice just this measure and the downbeat of the next measure, gradually increasing the tempo. This part may be omitted if you don't have enough tubes or if it is too difficult.

• **Measures 33–38**

Distribute the remaining accompaniment tubes to play measures 33–38:

> One student holds D and F
> One student holds Low B and G (or have intro players play this part also)
> One student holds E and C (or have intro players play this part also)
> One student holds A (or have the intro player play this part) and (opt.) Very Low C

Measures 33–35 are 3/4 measures. Feel free to play only the downbeat of these measures, which requires only F, G, and A tubes.

Using photocopied visuals or an overhead transparency, have students find the notes they will play and color-code them. This can be a note-learning exercise.

Practice slowly and gradually increase the tempo until you create a cut-time feel. You may want to point to the colored-in notes on an overhead projection to help your students know when to play (and when not to play).

Sing along if you like or perform with your school choir. A reproducible Lyric Sheet is provided.

I Don't Need Anything but You

(From *Annie*)

* Chord symbols are for teachers who may want to play along on piano or guitar to fill in harmonies.

** = 8vb; cap B tube or use bass tube; this is an optional note.

I Don't Need Anything but You - 2 - 1

C   Em   F/G   Em Dm   Cmaj7   F/G
round   your cute_ lit-tle   fin-ger.   You made_ life a
(echo) Soli
(8vb)
C   Em   F/G   Em Dm   C   Cmaj7
song,   Soli   You made_ me the   sing-er.   And what's that
(8vb)
C9   F   Fm6   C
bath-tub tune I   al-ways "Bub-buh-boo?"_   I don't need
(8vb)
Dm   C/G   Dm   F   D9   G7
an-y-thing,   an-y-thing,   an-y-thing.   I don't need   an-y-
loco   8vb   loco   8vb
F/G   G   Cmaj7   F/G   Cmaj7   F/G   G7C
thing   but   you!_   Ending:
Soli
(8vb)   loco (like intro.)   8vb
(+15mb if available)

Boomwhackers® Visual

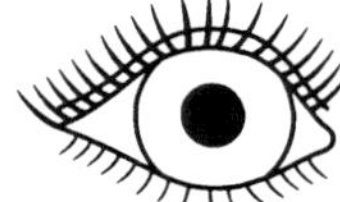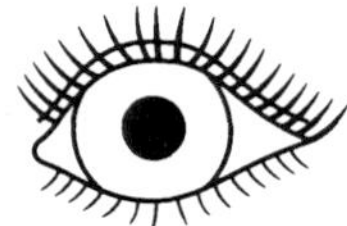

I Don't Need Anything but You

(From *Annie*)

Music by CHARLES STROUSE
Lyric by MARTIN CHARNIN

Copy for each student or use as an overhead transparency.
Color in the noteheads to match the tubes.

* ≡ = 8vb; cap B tube or use bass tube; this is an optional note.

Visual

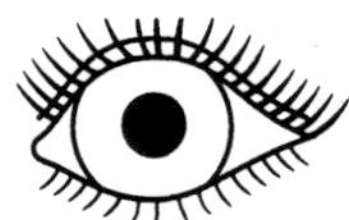

I Don't Need Anything but You

(From *Annie*)

Music by CHARLES STROUSE
Lyric by MARTIN CHARNIN

Lyric Sheet

Verse:
Together at last, together forever;
We're tying a knot they never can sever.
I don't need sunshine now to turn my skies to blue,
I don't need anything but you!
You wrapped me around your cute little finger.
You made life a song,
You made me the singer.
And what's that bathtub tune I always "Bub-buh-boo?"
I don't need anything, anything, anything.
I don't need anything but you!

Big Spender

Tubes required:

(Tubes are listed in order of occurrence in the music for each part. For the "Low" tubes, use bass tubes or tubes with Octavator™ caps. Suggested tube distribution appears in the teaching suggestions below.)

Melody: It is suggested that the melody be used from the CD or played on a keyboard instrument.

Accompaniment Patterns:

(Note that the entire Boomwhackers® part may be doubled up an octave.)

Pattern 1 (and Intro):	Low A	Low G
Pattern 2:	Low E	Low A
Pattern 3:	Low F	Low E
Pattern 4:	Low E	Low A

Tremolos (measures 7–8, 11, 15–16): Low F   Low B

Final Chord (tremolos): Low C, Low E, Low A (Pattern 4 players plus the Low C)

This piece requires only three diatonic Boomwhackers® sets, unless parts are doubled. Six students could play the entire accompaniment. Consider assigning simple rhythm patterns for unpitched percussion to some students and have others do movement, and then switch parts.

Teaching suggestions:

ACCOMPANIMENT PATTERNS

- Listen to the full performance CD several times and patsch along. Seat students with their pattern partners and in the order of the pitches they play:
  - One (or more) student(s) hold(s) Low A and Low G
  - One (or more) student(s) hold(s) Low E and Low A
  - One (or more) student(s) hold(s) Low F and Low E
  - One (or more) student(s) hold(s) Low E and Low A
- Teach each of the four patterns separately by rote. Pattern 2 players should also play the Low E on the downbeat of measure 9.
- Using photocopied visuals or an overhead transparency, have students find their notes or patterns and color-code them. This can be a note-learning exercise.

TREMOLOS (measures 7–8, 11, 15–16, and final chord)

- Distribute tubes to practice the tremolos in measures 7, 11, 15, 16, 18, 20, and the final measure:
  - One (or more) student(s) hold(s) two Low F tubes
  - One (or more) student(s) hold(s) two Low B tubes
  - One (or more) student(s) hold(s) two Low C tubes (plus the Low E and Low A Pattern 4 players)
  These notes are not part of any pattern. See the General Teaching Suggestions on page 2 for optional ways to play tremolos.
- Practice with the CD (full performance or accompaniment). You may want to point to the colored-in notes on an overhead projection to help your students know when to play and when to rest. Swing the eighth notes!

EXTENSION

Choose some students to play rainstick or shakers in measure 2 and, optionally, in the final measure. Students playing Patterns 2, 3, or 4, or the Low F and Low B tremolos have time to switch instruments.

Boomwhackers® Visual

Big Spender
(From *Sweet Charity*)

Music by CY COLEMAN
Lyric by DOROTHY FIELDS

Copy for each student or use as an overhead transparency.
Color in the noteheads to match the tubes.

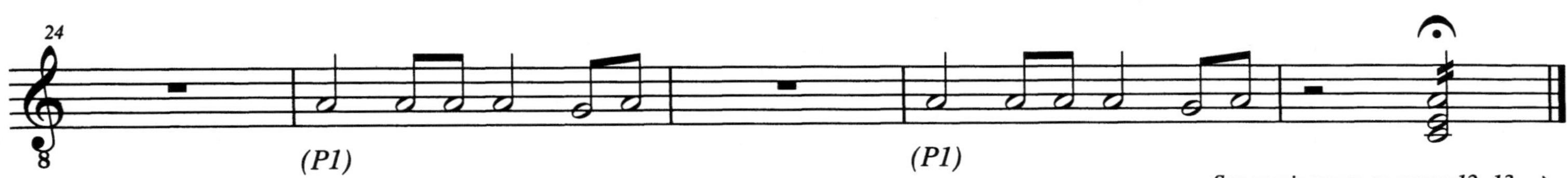

See music score on pages 12–13.→

* See ideas for tremolo techniques in General Teaching Suggestions, page 2.

Big Spender

(From *Sweet Charity*)

When using CD, wait for 4 clicks.

Music by CY COLEMAN
Lyric by DOROTHY FIELDS

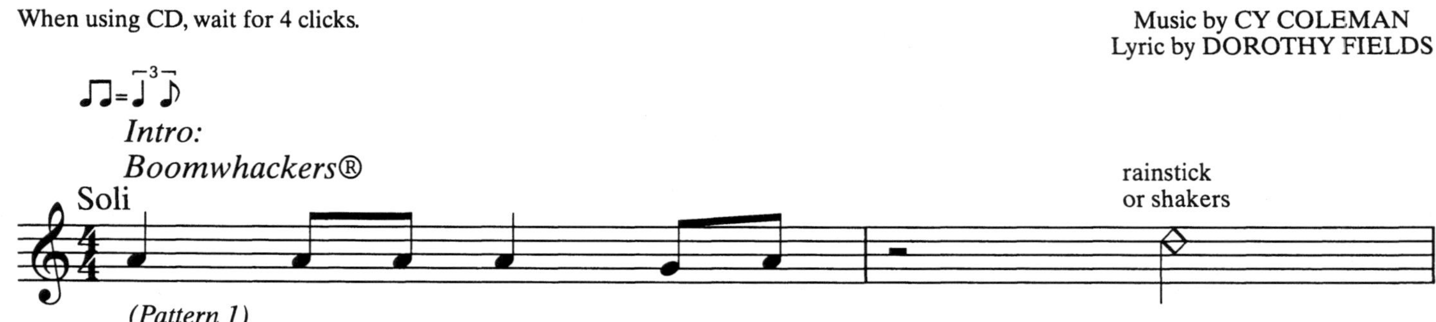

* Chord symbols are for teachers who may want to play along on piano or guitar to fill in harmonies.
** See ideas for tremolo techniques in General Teaching Suggestions, page 2.

Big Spender - 2 - 1

12
E7(♯5)
3
Am
(P3)
(P2)
(P2)
8
15 F
B7
Am
Soli
(P4)
8
19
F9
(P4)
(P3)
8
22 E9
Am
Soli
(P1)
8
25
Am6(9)
(P1)
(P1)
8
Optional:
Add shakers or rainsticks.

Applause

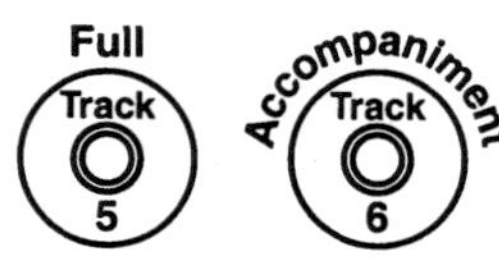

Tubes required:

(Tubes are listed in order of occurrence in the music for each part. For the "Low" tubes, use bass tubes or tubes with Octavator™ caps. Suggested tube distribution appears in the teaching suggestions below.)

Boomwhacker® Parts (Introduction, Soli, and Accompaniment):

Low C   Low D   Low E   Low F   Low G   C   D   Low A   (opt.: Low B♭)   F

Melody: It is suggested that the melody be used from the CD or played on a keyboard instrument.

Teaching suggestions:

Distribute tubes, seating the soli, intro, and accompaniment players in their groups:
   One (or more) student(s) hold(s) Low C and Low D
   One (or more) student(s) hold(s) Low E and Low F
   One (or more) student(s) hold(s) Low A and Low G
   One (or more) student(s) hold(s) two Low F tubes
   One student holds Low C and C, and (opt.) Low B♭
   (see music for optional notes if you do not have chromatic tubes)

ACCOMPANIMENT (with four quarter notes per measure)
- First work on all the measures with four quarter notes, having all the students with the Low F, C, D, Low D, and Low G tubes find their notes on their visual and color in their notes.
- Then have students play along with the full performance CD as you cue their parts. Anyone not playing can look at the Lyric Sheet (see page 18) and sing along softly.

INTRODUCTION and SOLI PARTS
- Next, work out the introduction and soli parts. The eighth notes in measures 2 and 4 may be omitted; it will be easier to teach them if the same student holds both the Low F and Low D tubes.
- To simplify measure 25 and avoid the chromatic tube, Low G may be substituted for the B♭.
- Notice that the soli at the end (measure 36) is like the introduction until the final measure.
- Slow down the tempo to work out these sections, color-coding the visuals and cueing the students as needed.

MEASURES 20–21 and 34–36
You're almost done! The only measures still to work out are measures 20–21, and 34–downbeat of 36, and the last measure.
- To teach measures 20–21 where Low C and C play together in octaves, have the class identify the rhythm:
       TA rest rest TA   rest rest TA TA
Speak the rhythm and then play it together. For this exercise, students may play whatever tube they are holding. Repeat, having only the players with the correct tubes play the part as shown in the music. Listen to the CD and then try to play along with the CD. Add singing and explain how the tubes echo the voice in measure 21.
- Teach measures 34–downbeat of 36 in the same way, by having the class identify and speak the rhythm as "TA rest rest TA TA rest rest TA TA." Play the rhythm on whatever tubes the students are holding. Repeat, with only the players holding the correctly pitched tubes. Listen to the CD and then play along with it.

FINAL MEASURE
Practice the final measure (three Low F quarter notes), having the class shout "Applause!" as shown in the music. Add singing. This is a great performance showstopper!

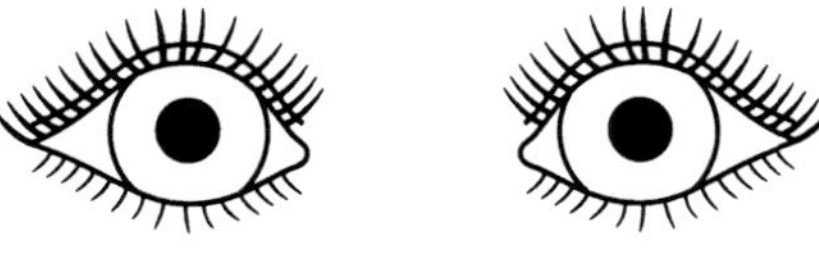

Applause

(From *Applause*)

Music by CHARLES STROUSE
Lyric by LEE ADAMS

Copy for each student or use as an overhead transparency.
Color in the noteheads to match the tubes.

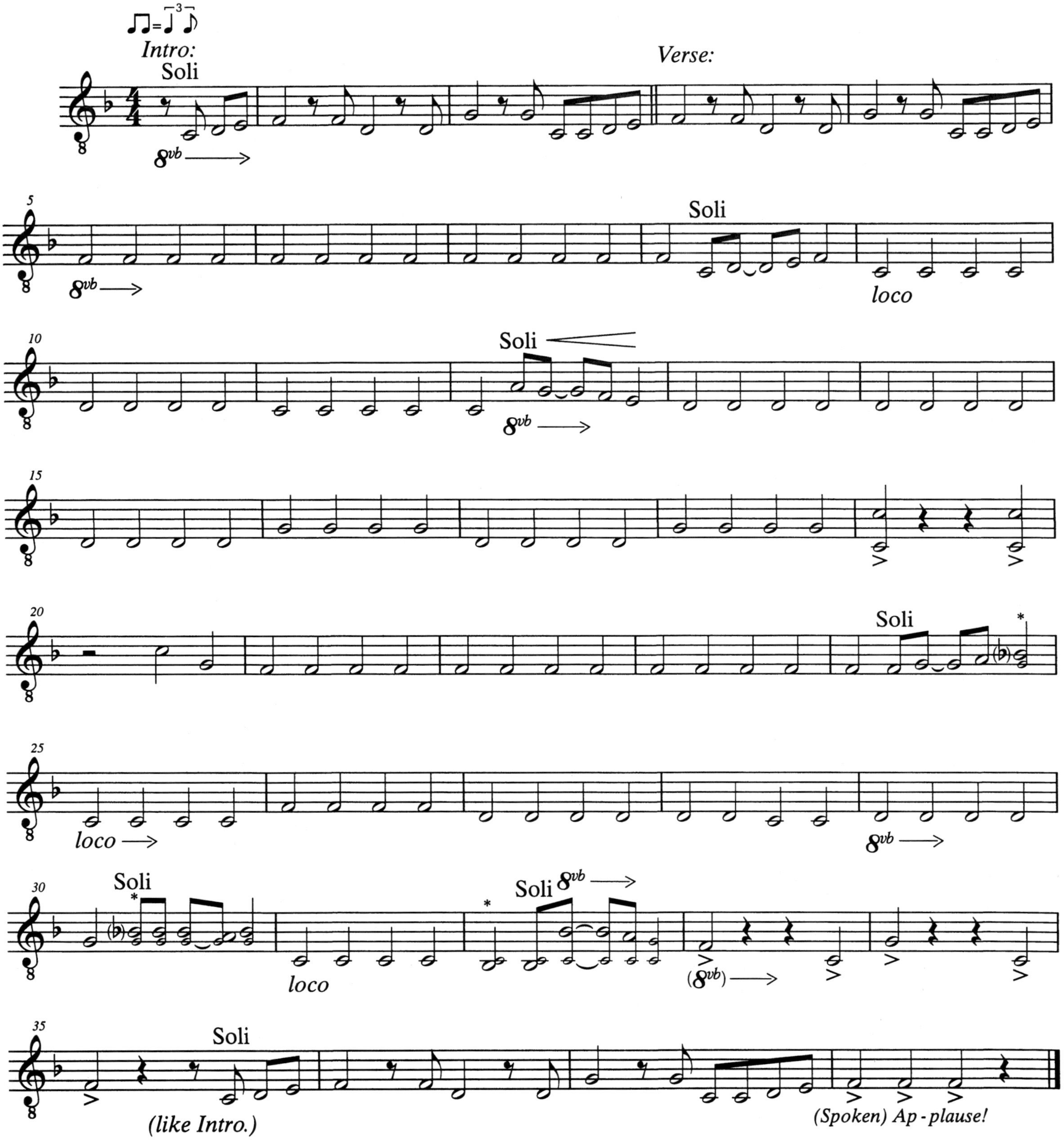
Intro:
Soli
Verse:
8vb
Soli
loco
Soli
8vb
Soli
loco
8vb
Soli
loco
Soli 8vb
(8vb)
Soli
(like Intro.)
(Spoken) Ap-plause!

* Cue notes are an option if you don't have a B♭ tube.

See music score on pages 16–17.⟶

Applause

(From *Applause*)

Music by CHARLES STROUSE
Lyric by LEE ADAMS

* Chord symbols are for teachers who may want to play along on piano or guitar to fill in harmonies.

* Cue notes are an option if you don't have a B♭ tube.

Applause - 2 - 2

Visual

Applause

(From *Applause*)

Music by CHARLES STROUSE
Lyric by LEE ADAMS

Lyric Sheet

Verse:
What is it that we're living for?
Applause, Applause!
Nothing I know brings on the glow
Like sweet applause.
You're thinking you're through,
That nobody cares,
Then suddenly, you hear it starting!
And somehow you're in charge again,
And it's a ball.
Trumpets all sing,
Life seems to swing,
And you're the king of it all,
'Cause you've had a taste of
The sound that says love,
Applause, Applause, Applause!
(Spoken) Applause!

Aquarius

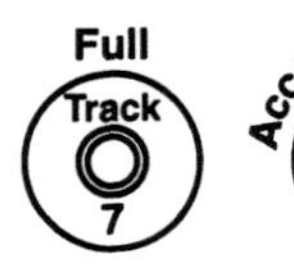

Tubes required:

(Tubes are listed in order of occurrence in the music for each part. For the "Low" tubes, use bass tubes or tubes with Octavator™ caps. Suggested tube distribution appears in the teaching suggestions below.)

Accompaniment Patterns:

Pattern 1 (and Intro):   Low D   Low A
Pattern 2:   Low G   Low D
(Low C—only for downbeat of measure 19; it is optional because it is doubled in the Boomwhackers® melody part up an octave.)
Pattern 3:   Low E   Low A
Pattern 4:   Low F   Low A

Melody (starting in measure 4)—**Optional:**   Low A   Low B   C   D   Low G

Boomwhackers® Accompaniment Part (measure 19 to end):
C   D   E   D, F   D, G   D, A   F, G   F   G   (opt.: Low A)   (opt.: Low D, Low A)

(Notes separated by commas appear as chords in the music. However, you don't necessarily have to distribute both tubes in a chord to the same student. See suggested distribution in teaching suggestions below.)

Teaching suggestions:

Listen to the full performance CD several times and sway to the music, hippie-style!

ACCOMPANIMENT PATTERNS

- Distribute the required tubes to teach the Intro/Pattern 1 and other three patterns first. Each pattern can be played by one student. Seat children according to the patterns they will play.
- The four easy patterns may be taught by rote, or you may use the visual on pages 24–25 as a transparency or photocopied sheets and have students color-code their notes if you are focusing on note-reading.
- Practice with the CD (full performance or accompaniment track) and cue the pattern groups. Have the rest of the class use their lyric sheets (see page 21) to sing along softly. Singers will need to ignore the *8vb* indications shown in the music.

MELODY

- You may want to add the melody on Boomwhackers® (measures 4–downbeat of 19) at this point. However, there are several other options: You or a student could also play the part on a keyboard or Orff barred instrument; if you use a keyboard, change the tremolos to standard trills. Playing on a recorder is another option if you ignore the *8vb* indication.
- If you do choose to try the melody on tubes, you need only five different tubes:
  One student holds one or two D tubes
  One student holds Low A and Low G
  One student holds two Low B and C
  C, Low A, and Low B players will play tremolos on these pitches. See General Teaching Suggestions on page 2 for tremolo techniques.
- Since the melodic movement is all stepwise, give students the starting pitch "A," and see if they can figure out the melody by ear. Making sure students can sing the melody at this point, play each pitch slowly on a keyboard or other instrument and have students guess what pitches come next.

- Choose five (or ten; two for each pitch) melody players to sit in scale degree order, Low G to D.
- Put pattern and melody parts together from intro to downbeat of measure 19.
- In measure 19, the melody occurs on the CD (both tracks) as a keyboard solo to the end of the piece. Explain the Boomwhackers® chords that accompany this melody in measures 21 to the end. Looking at the visual (page 25), practice patsching or clapping the rhythms of the chords only from here to the end. Transfer to the Boomwhackers®, cueing the students as needed.

ACCOMPANIMENT PART (measure 19 to end)

- Distribute tubes:
    - One student holds D and F
    - One student holds D and A
    - One student holds D and G
    - One student holds C and E
- (Low D and Low A are used only in the last three measures, and the regular D and A up an octave may be substituted.)
- Measures 19–20 double the melody and measures 27–28 echo the melody (see the music). These measures could be assigned to the same five students who played the melody part in measure 4.
- It would also be fun for the class to use their ears and guess these pitches. Give them the starting pitch of "C," play the pitches (measure 19, beat 2–measure 20) slowly and see if they can guess the pitches. Repeat with measure 27, beat 4–measure 28.

ENDING

Teach the last three measures with D, Low A, and Low D by rote.
Wear tie-dyed shirts and perform for the school! What's your zodiac sign?!

Aquarius

(From *Hair*)

Music by GALT MacDERMOT
Words by JAMES RADO and GEROME RAGNI

Lyric Sheet

Verse:
When the moon is in the seventh house,
And Jupiter aligns with Mars,
Then peace will guide the planets,
And love will steer the stars;

Chorus:
This is the dawning of the age of Aquarius,
The age of Aquarius, Aquarius, Aquarius.

See music score on pages 22–23. →

Aquarius

(From *Hair*)

When using CD, wait for 4 clicks.

Music by GALT MacDERMOT
Words by JAMES RADO and GEROME RAGNI

* Chord symbols are for teachers who may want to play along on piano or guitar to fill in harmonies.
** See ideas for tremolo techniques in General Teaching Suggestions, page 2.

Aquarius - 2 - 1

F
G7
And love
will steer the
(8vb)
(P4)
(P2)
Chorus:
Bb
N.C.
Keyboard solo to end (occurs on both CD tracks)
(8vb) loco
stars; this is the dawn - ing of the age of A -
(8vb) loco
quar - i - us, the age of A - quar - i - us,
Dm
G7
A - quar - i - us,
Echo
A -
Dm
Ending:
quar - i - us.
opt. 8vb
loco opt. 8vb

Boomwhackers®
Visual

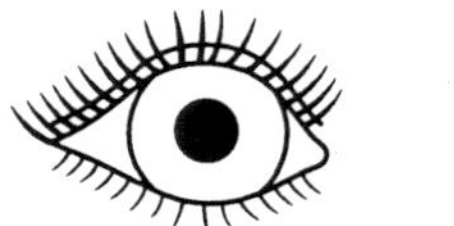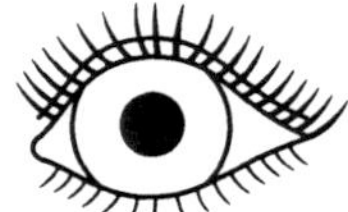

Aquarius
(From *Hair*)

Music by GALT MacDERMOT
Words by JAMES RADO and GEROME RAGNI

Copy for each student or use as an overhead transparency.
Color in the noteheads to match the tubes.

Intro:
Boomwhackers®

Melody
(Play on Boomwhackers®
or keyboard or use CD.)

Verse:

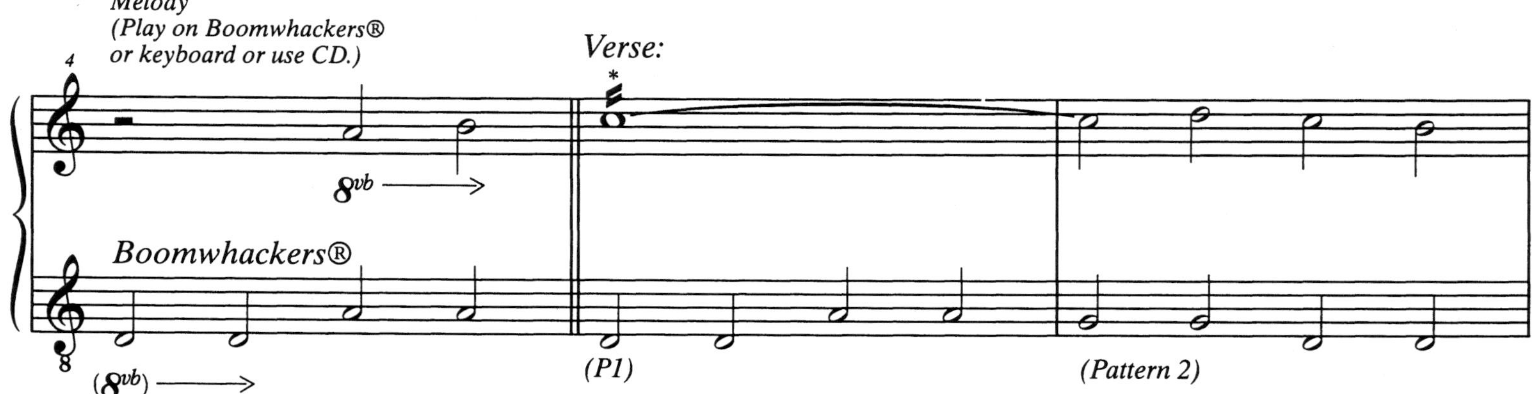

* See ideas for tremolo techniques in General Teaching Suggestions, page 2.

Aquarius - 2 - 1

13
(8vb)
(8vb)
(P2)
(P3)
16
(8vb)
(8vb)
(P4)
(P2)
loco
20
Chorus:
23
26
Echo
29
32 Ending:
8vb
loco
8vb

Kids!

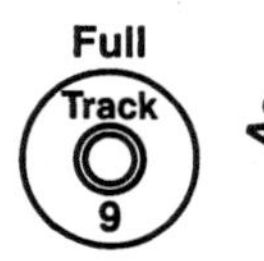

Tubes required:

(Tubes are listed in order of occurrence in the music for each part. For the "Low" tubes, use bass tubes or tubes with Octavator™ caps. Suggested tube distribution appears in the teaching suggestions below.)

Intro: High CB   A   E   G   F   E   D

Melody: High CA   G   E   D   F

Accompaniment: C   D   E   F   G   Low B Low F Low E Low D Low C Low A Low G

Teaching suggestions:

- Listen to the full performance CD track and patsch the steady beat to become familiar with the song. Talk about the lyrics and the form of the piece. Use the lyric sheet and have fun singing the song with the CD.
- Have all students clap the following rhythm:

- Look at the music score (bottom line) to see where this pattern occurs in the accompaniment: measures 8, 12, 16, 24, 28, and 32.

ACCOMPANIMENT

- Teach the **A** Section accompaniment (bottom part) first, having other students sing the melody softly. Use the Lyric Sheet on page 32.
- The accompaniment may be taught by rote or by using the visual (see page 30).
- Distribute tubes for the **A** Section:
    - One student holds 2 C tubes
    - One student holds D and E
    - One student holds F and G
    - One student holds A (preferably 2 A tubes due to the repeated notes)
    - One student holds B (1 or 2)
    - One student holds Low F (1 or 2)
    - One student holds High C
- Teach the **B** Section accompaniment.
- Distribute tubes for the **B** Section:
    - One student holds 2 Low E tubes
    - One student holds 2 Low A tubes
    - (Same student from **A** Section can play the C tubes)
    - One student holds Low B and Low G

A SECTION MELODY

- Consider singing the melody or having a good keyboard student play it throughout the piece.
- Seat the melody players opposite the accompaniment players.
- Distribute tubes for the **A** Section Melody:
    - One student holds High C and B
    - One student holds B and A
    - One student holds G and F

One student holds E and D
One student holds G and A
(This distribution is based on eighth-note patterns.)
- Use the Intro and Melody Visual (see page 31) to have students color-code their notes and mark the parts they will play. If available, use music stands to place their visuals.
- Practice only the **A** sections (measures 5–12 and 21–36).
- Notice that the **A** section melody repeats but changes in measure 27 to the end.

B SECTION MELODY
- The **B** section melody in measures 13–16 should be played on a keyboard instrument, or use the accompaniment CD track, which includes this part.
- Measures 17–18 are identical and can be taught by rote, but also use the Intro and Melody Visual so students can see where their parts occur.
- Clap the rhythms in measures 19–20 before transferring to the tubes.

INTRO and CODA
- Finally, teach the intro, with all students clapping the rhythms first. The intro players should be the same as the melody players.
- Put the whole song together, playing first with the full performance CD track and then with the accompaniment CD track.

Kids!

(From *Bye, Bye Birdie*)

When using CD, wait for 6 clicks.

Music by CHARLES STROUSE
Words by LEE ADAMS

* Chord symbols are for teachers who may want to play along on piano or guitar to fill in harmonies.

Kids! - 2 - 1

Boomwhackers®
Swing 8ths
Am7 D7 Am7 D7 Dm7 G7 G7(♯5)
Nois - y cra - zy slop - py la - zy loaf - ers!__ While we're on the sub - ject:
I don't see why an - y - bod - y wants 'em!__ Why are they so dread - ful?
loco
8vb
A
C C6 Cmaj7 C6
Kids! You can talk and talk__ till your face is blue!
Kids! They are just im - pos - si - ble to con - trol!
loco
C7 F E F6 E F6
Kids! But they still do just__ what they want to do!
Kids! With their aw - ful clothes_ and their rock and roll!
8vb
F B7(♯5) B7 Em7 A7
Why can't they be like we were, per - fect in ev - 'ry way?
(8vb)
F6 D9 G7 C6 G7 C
What's the mat - ter with kids to - day?
(8vb)

Boomwhackers® Visual

Accompaniment

Kids!

(From *Bye, Bye Birdie*)

Music by CHARLES STROUSE
Words by LEE ADAMS

Copy for each student or use as an overhead transparency.
Color in the noteheads to match the tubes.

Boomwhackers®
Visual

Kids!

(From *Bye, Bye Birdie*)

Intro and Melody

Music by CHARLES STROUSE
Words by LEE ADAMS

Copy for each student or use as an overhead transparency.
Color in the noteheads to match the tubes.

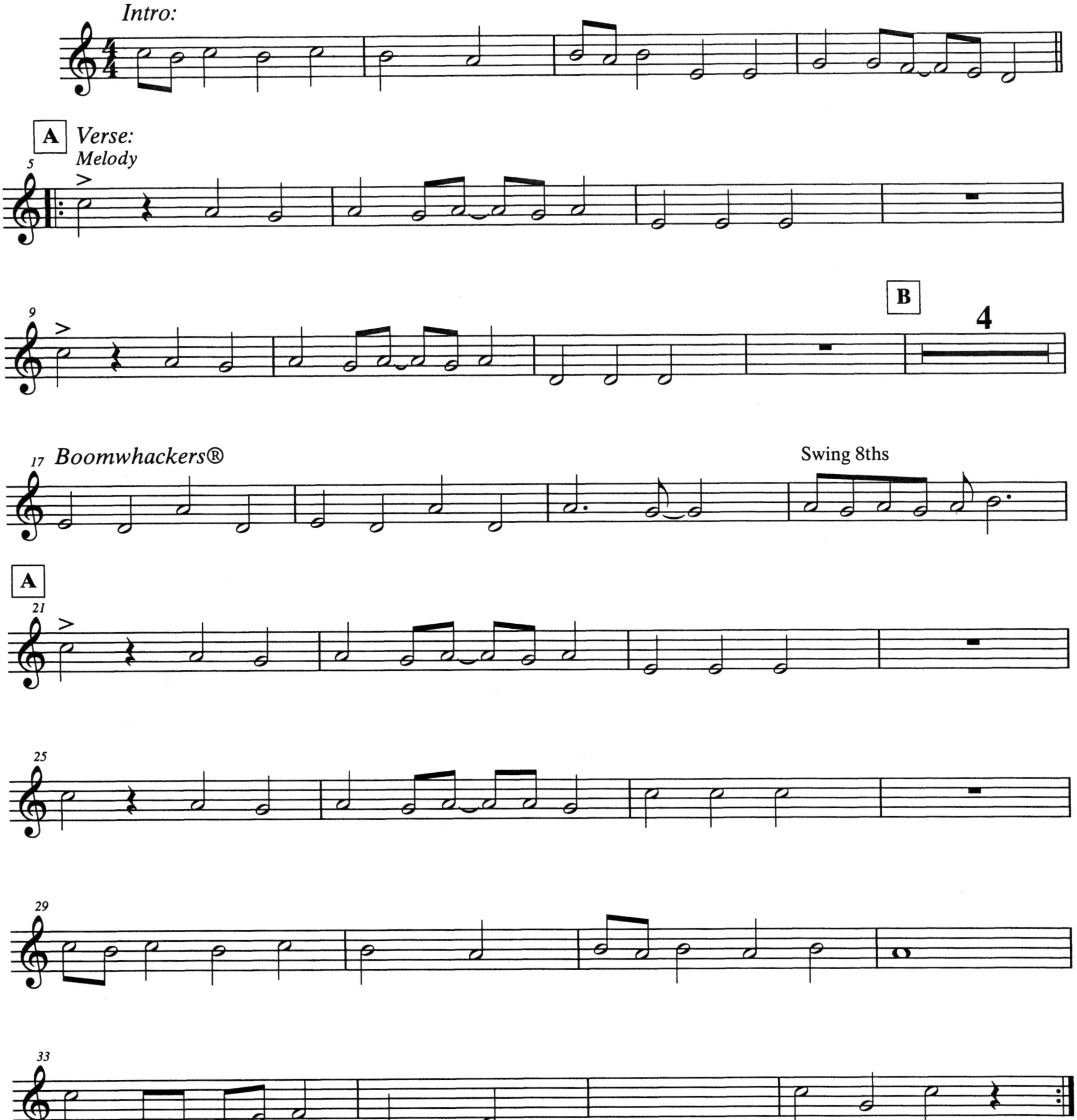

Visual

Kids!

(From *Bye, Bye Birdie*)

Music by CHARLES STROUSE
Words by LEE ADAMS

Lyric Sheet

Verse 1:
Kids! I don't know what's wrong with these kids today!
Kids! Who can understand anything they say?
Kids! They are disobedient, disrespectful oafs!
Noisy crazy sloppy lazy loafers!
While we're on the subject:
Kids! You can talk and talk till your face is blue!
Kids! But they still do just what they want to do!
Why can't they be like we were, perfect in ev'ry way?
What's the matter with kids today?

Verse 2:
Kids! I don't know what's wrong with these kids today!
Even I don't understand what they say!
Kids! They are so ridiculous and so immature!
I don't see why anybody wants 'em!
Why are they so dreadful?
Kids! They are just impossible to control!
Kids! With their awful clothes and their rock and roll!
Why can't they be like we were, perfect in ev'ry way?
What's the matter with kids today?

Day by Day

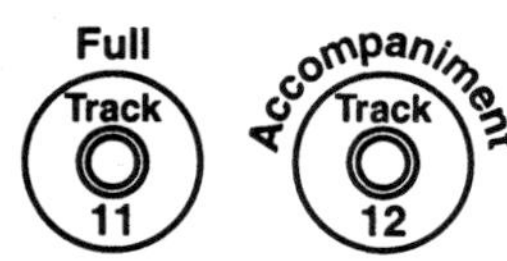

Tubes required:

(Tubes are listed in order of occurrence in the music for each part. For the "Low" tubes, use bass tubes or tubes with Octavator™ caps. Suggested tube distribution appears in the teaching suggestions below.)

Melody (top line of music score):   Low B   Low G   Low A   D   E   C

Accompaniment Patterns (middle line of music score):
Pattern 1 (and Intro; 2 measures):   D   E   C
Pattern 2 (one measure):   E   F
Pattern 3 (one measure):   D   E
Pattern 4 (one measure):   Low B
Pattern 5 (one measure):   Low A   Low G
Pattern 6 (one measure):   Low A   Low B
Pattern 7 (one measure):   Low G   Low A

Ending (middle line of music score): E (opt.: G♯, D♯)

Bass Part (bottom line of music score):   Low C   Low F   Low E   Low D   Low B   Low G

Teaching suggestions:

Listen to the full performance CD track and conduct a three-beat waltz pattern in the air to become familiar with the song or patsch-clap-clap to the three-beat pattern.

BASS PART
- Show the visual (see page 35) with the chord symbols and discuss how the bass part is usually just the root of the chord, except when the chord symbol shows a slash followed by another note; then the note after the slash is the Boomwhackers® bass part.
- Using the visual, color-code the notes to teach the bass part (bottom line of score) first to all students.
- Distribute tubes:
  - One student holds Low C and Low F
  - One student holds Low E and Low D
  - One student holds Low B and Low G
- Play just the bass part along with the full performance CD Track 11.

MELODY (begins in measure 5)
- The melody part is difficult and optional. It is preferable to use CD Track 11 or have the melody played on a keyboard or barred Orff instrument, adjusting octaves if needed.
- If you want to try the melody on Boomwhackers®, listen to it on the CD and hum along. Distribute tubes and then teach this part with the visual (see page 39), color-coding the notes:
  - One student holds two Low A tubes
  - One student holds Low B and Low G
  - One student holds Low A and D
  - One student holds D and E
  - One student holds C and Low B
- Practice the tremolos on Low A and Low B. See the General Teaching Suggestions on page 2 for tremolo techniques.
- Using the melody and bass visuals, combine the melody with the bass part.

ACCOMPANIMENT

- Accompaniment Pattern 1 is a TWO-measure pattern. Be sure to seat these D, E, and C players together.
- Distribute tubes:
    One student holds C and D
    One student holds E and D (this student could also play Pattern 3)
- All other patterns are only one measure, and each can be played by one student. All seven patterns could be played by only five students. (Pattern 3 can be played by the E and D Pattern 1 player; Pattern 6 player could also play Pattern 4; Pattern 5 player could also play Pattern 7.) Teach these by rote, seating players for each pattern together and using the form visual (see page 38) to put the patterns in the correct order.
- The final Emaj7 chord has optional G♯ and D♯ tubes, which sound cool if you have the chromatic tubes. Pattern 3 players can just complete the song with their E tubes.
- Put all parts together, using visuals as needed. Try playing with the accompaniment CD Track 12.

Boomwhackers® Visual

Day by Day

(From *Godspell*)

Bass Part

Words and Music by
STEPHEN SCHWARTZ

Copy for each student or use as an overhead transparency.
Color in the noteheads to match the tubes.

Easy waltz

* See ideas for tremolo techniques in General Teaching Suggestions, page 2.

See music score on pages 36–37. ⟶

Day by Day

(From *Godspell*)

When using CD, wait for 3 clicks.

Words and Music by
STEPHEN SCHWARTZ

Easy waltz

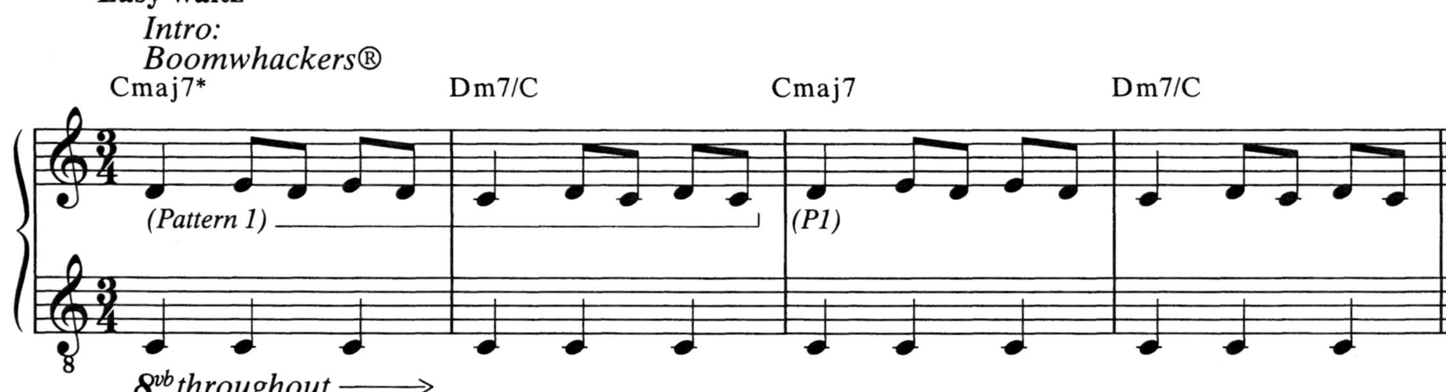

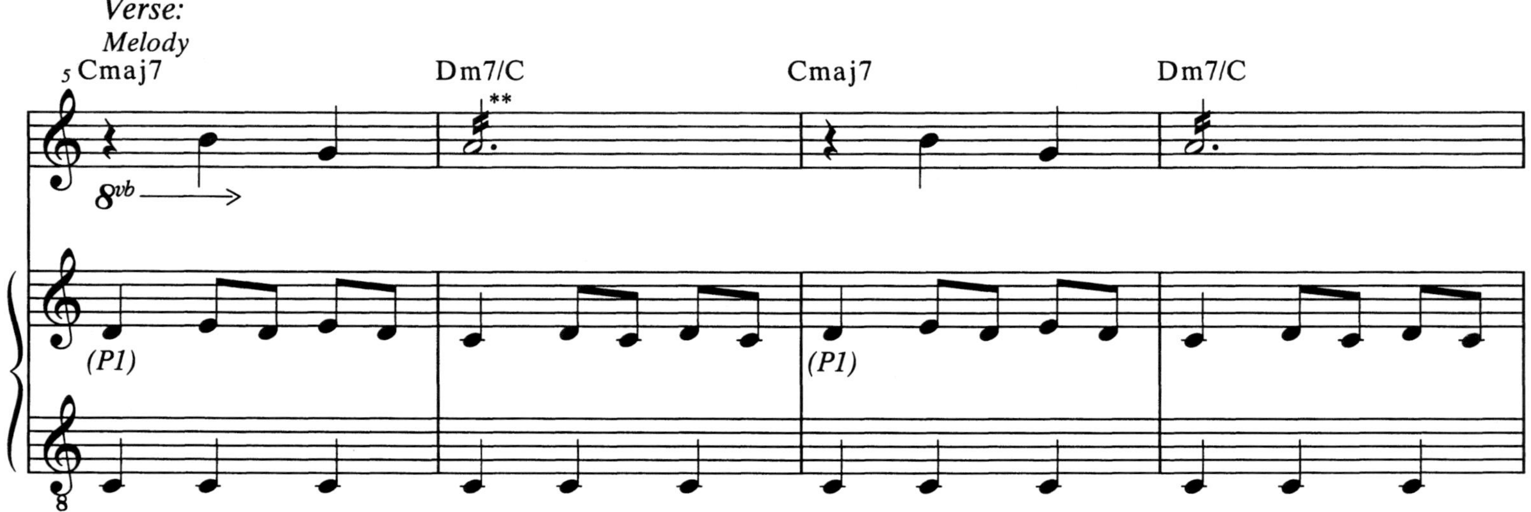

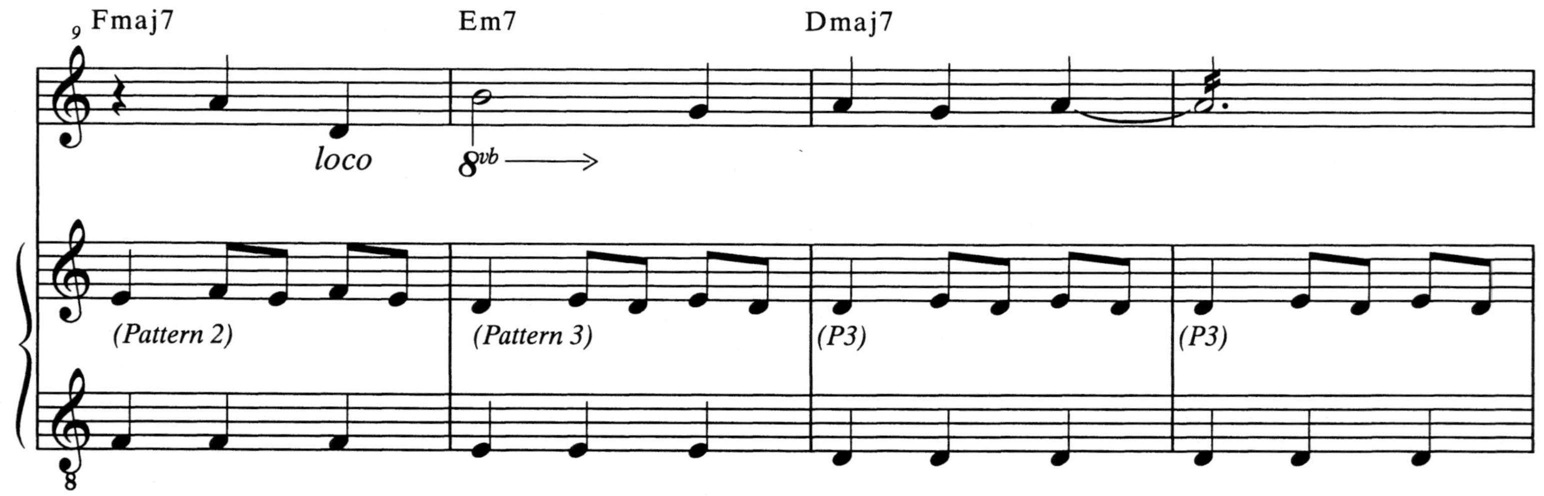

* Chord symbols are for teachers who may want to play along on piano or guitar to fill in harmonies.
** See ideas for tremolo techniques in General Teaching Suggestions, page 2.

Day by Day - 2 - 1

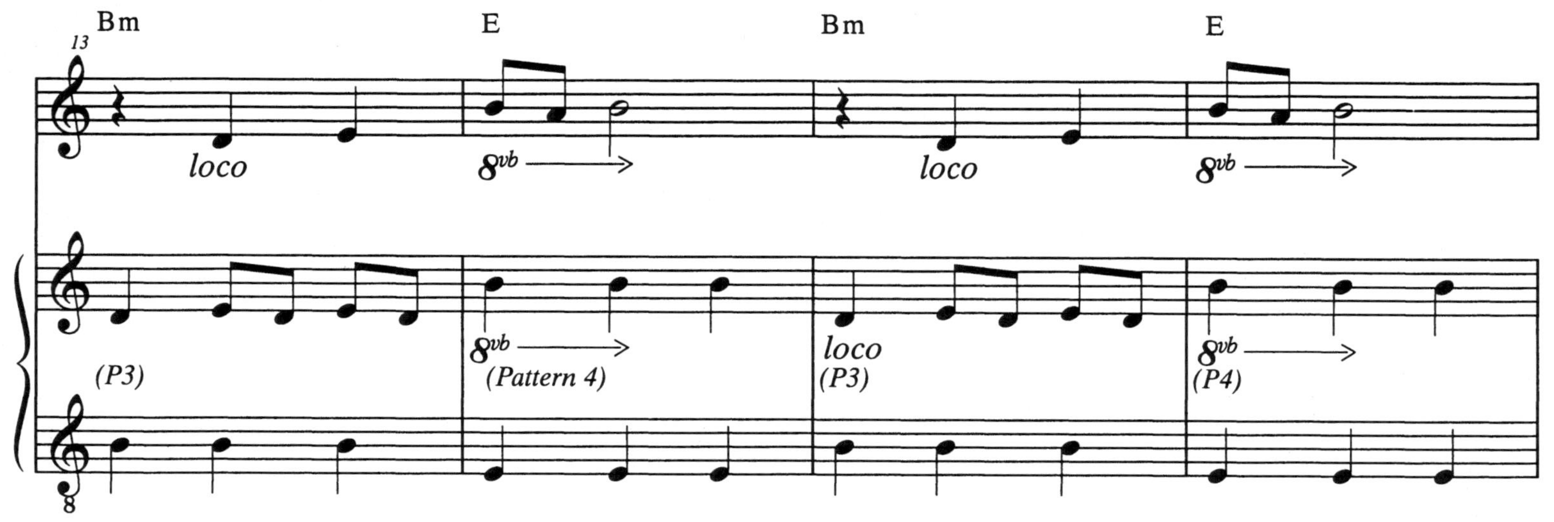

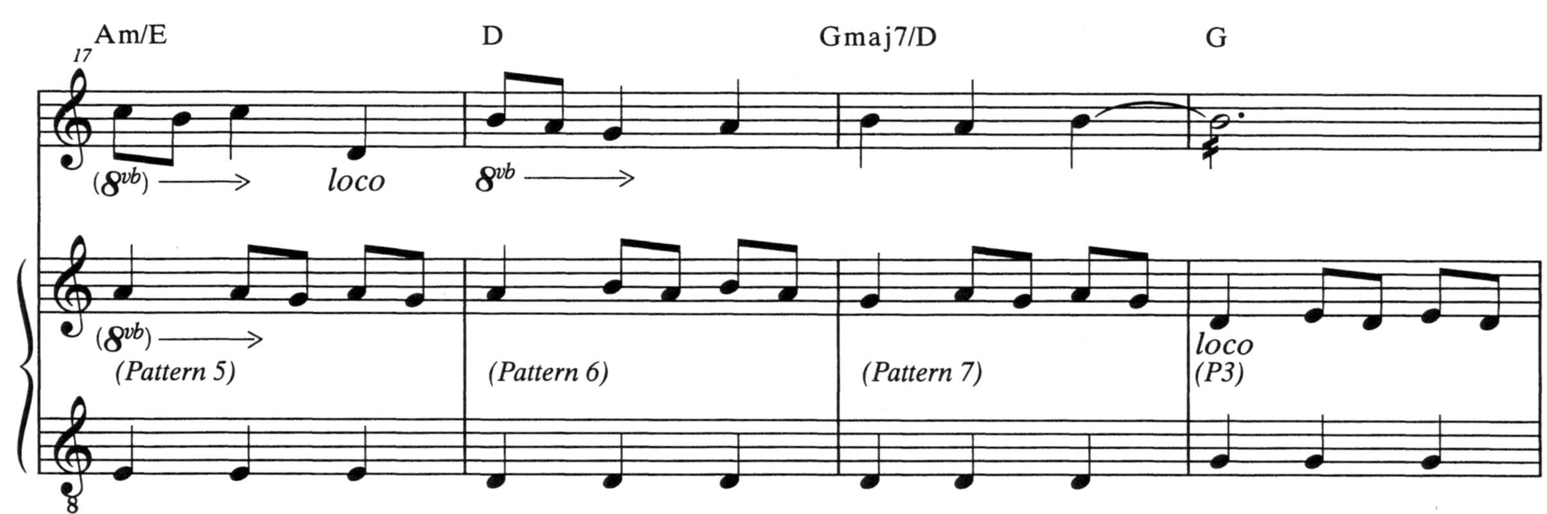

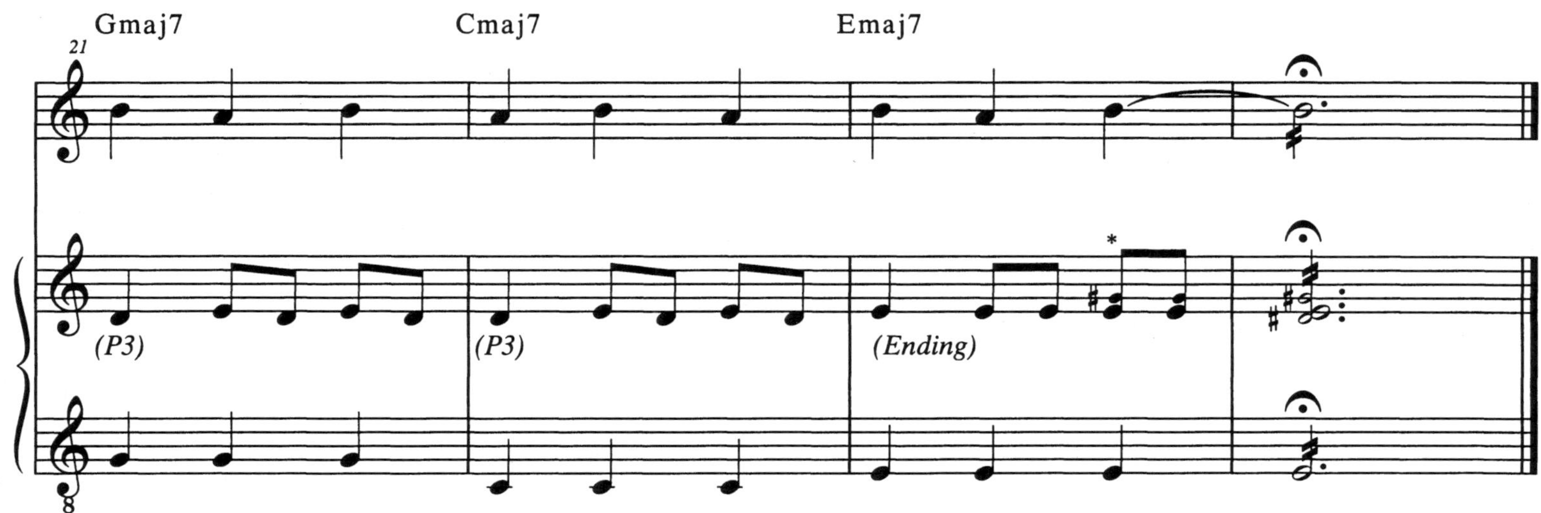

* Accidentals require chromatic tubes and are optional.

Day by Day - 2 - 2

Form Visual

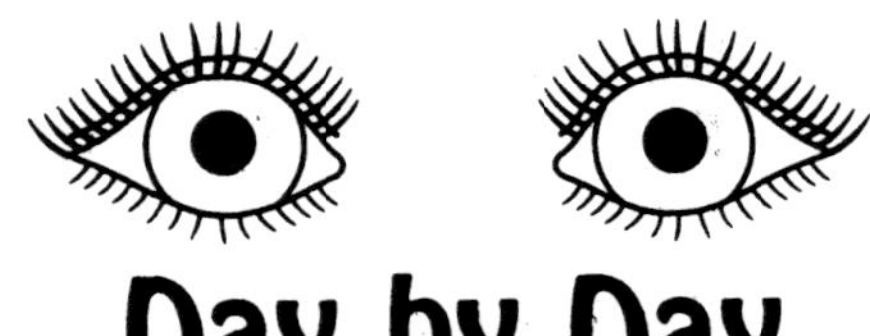

Day by Day

(From *Godspell*)

Patterns

Words and Music by
STEPHEN SCHWARTZ

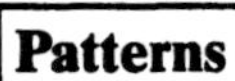

Copy for each student or use as an overhead transparency.

Easy waltz

Intro: $\frac{3}{4}$

Pattern 1		P1	

5 *Verse:*

P1		P1	

9

Pattern 2	Pattern 3	P3	P3

13

P3	Pattern 4	P3	P4

17

P5	P6	P7	P3

21

P3	P3	Ending	

**Boomwhackers®
Visual**

Day by Day
(From *Godspell*)

Words and Music by
STEPHEN SCHWARTZ

Intro and Melody

Copy for each student or use as an overhead transparency.
Color in the noteheads to match the tubes.

Easy waltz

* See ideas for tremolo techniques in General Teaching Suggestions, page 2.

Hernando's Hideaway

Tubes required:

(Tubes are listed in order of occurrence in the music for each part. For the "Low" tubes, use bass tubes or tubes with Octavator™ caps. Suggested tube distribution appears in the teaching suggestions below.)

Intro: F   E   D   C   Low B   Low A

Melody: F   E   (opt.: G♯)   B   A   High C   D   C   Low B   Low E   Low A

Accompaniment Patterns:
Pattern 1:   Low A   Low E   C
(Note the Pattern 1 rhythm changes in measure 7 to straight quarter notes.)
Pattern 2:   Low B   Low E   (opt.: Low G♯)

Teaching suggestions:

- Discuss the tango. The tango is a Latin-American ballroom dance in 2/4 or 4/4 time, or the music for this dance. *Tango* is also a verb; let's tango! The tango was originally an African drum dance, possibly of Niger-Congo origin.

ACCOMPANIMENT
- Play the full performance CD for "Hernando's Hideaway." Listen to the tango style and patsch the accompaniment rhythm in measure 3 throughout the song except on "Hernando's Hideaway!" and "Olay!" Repeat, but this time shout "Hernando's Hideaway!" and "Olay!" with the recording.
- There are only two accompaniment patterns. Students could play just the two accompaniment patterns with the CD and sound great! Note the rhythm change to straight quarter notes in measure 5. Teach these two patterns to the entire class. Low G♯ is the preferred note to Low B for beat 3 of Pattern 2.
- Teach the "A" on the downbeat of measures 11 and 19 just before "Hernando's Hideaway!" Have the Pattern 1 players all play their A tubes.
- Teach the "Olay!" measures 12 and first and second endings, with Pattern 1 players playing their E and A tubes. Write the pattern order on the board:

Pattern Order (starting in measure 3):

P1	**P1**	**P2**	**P2**	**P1**	**P1**	**P2**	**P2**	**"A" from P1 on downbeat**
"O-lay" = E-A	**P2**	**P2**	**P1**	**P1**	**P2**	**P2**		
"A" from P1 on downbeat		**"O-lay" = E-A**	*(repeat)*					

INTRO and MELODY
- If you like, add the intro and melody, played staccato on keyboard, or teach it on the tubes using the visual (see page 42), color-coding the notes and omitting the sixteenth notes.
- Add castanets, claves, or woodblock on the steady beat.
- Add tambourine on "Olay!"
- Try playing with the accompaniment CD Track 14, which adds guitar, keyboard, bass, and drums.

Hernando's Hideaway

(From *The Pajama Game*)

When using CD, wait for 4 clicks.

Words and Music by
RICHARD ADLER and JERRY ROSS

* Chord symbols are for teachers who may want to play along on piano or guitar to fill in harmonies.
** May omit G♯; B is an option in Pattern 2.
† Olé! is spelled "Olay!" on original sheet music.

Boomwhackers® Visual

Hernando's Hideaway

(From *The Pajama Game*)

Words and Music by
RICHARD ADLER and JERRY ROSS

Melody

Copy for each student or use as an overhead transparency.
Color in the noteheads to match the tubes.

* May omit G#; B is an option in Pattern 2.
** Olé! is spelled "Olay!" on original sheet music.

If I Were a Rich Man

Tubes required:

(Tubes are listed in order of occurrence in the music for each part. For the "Low" tubes, use bass tubes or tubes with Octavator™ caps. Suggested tube distribution appears in the teaching suggestions below.)

Accompaniment Patterns:

Pattern 1 (and Intro):		Low C	Low E		
Pattern 2:	Low D	Low B	Low G		
Pattern 3:	Low C	Low G			
Pattern 4:	Low C	Low A			
Ending Pattern:	Low A	Low B	Low G	C	Low C

Melody: G F E C B♭ A♭ G♭ E♭ D G Low B

Teaching suggestions:

- Listen to the full performance CD track and patsch the accompaniment pattern rhythm to become familiar with the song.
- Use the lyric sheet (see bottom of page 44) to learn the song, first speaking the unusual syllables.
- Sing the song with the full performance CD Track 15.

ACCOMPANIMENT

- Teach the four accompaniment patterns by rote, seating players with their pattern partners.
- Distribute tubes for Pattern 1:
    - One student holds Low C
    - One student holds two Low E tubes
- Distribute tubes for Pattern 2:
    - One student holds Low D and Low G
    - One student holds two Low B tubes
- Distribute tubes for Pattern 3:
    - One student holds Low C
    - One student holds two Low G tubes
- Distribute tubes for Pattern 4:
    - One student holds Low C
    - One student holds two Low A tubes

ENDING

- Ending Pattern: Most of these notes are in other patterns, but it will be easier to assign one special group to play this part.
- Distribute tubes:
    - One student holds two Low A tubes
    - One student holds Low B and Low G
    - One student holds C and Low C
- Teach the Ending Pattern by rote.
- Copy the pattern order onto the board to put the parts together.

Pattern Order (starting with the intro):

P1	P1	P1	P1	P1	P1	P2	P3	P4	P2
P1	P1	P1	P1	P2	P3	Ending Pattern			

MELODY

- All students should sing throughout once they know the words.
- The Boomwhackers® melody requires B♭, A♭, G♭, and E♭ chromatic tubes and may be too difficult. Feel free to use the melody on the CD or play it on a keyboard instrument. You may also teach it using the melody visual and color-coding the notes.

EXTENSION

Add tambourine; shake on beats 1 and 3; hit on beats 2 and 4.

Visual

If I Were a Rich Man

(From *Fiddler on the Roof*)

Music by JERRY BOCK
Lyrics by SHELDON HARNICK

Lyric Sheet

If I were a rich man,
Daidle, deedle, daidle,
Digguh, digguh, deedle,
Daidle, dum.
All day long
I'd biddy, biddy bum,
If I were a wealthy man.
Wouldn't have to work hard,
Daidle, deedle, daidle,
Digguh, digguh, deedle,
Daidle, dum.
If I were a biddy,
Biddy rich, digguh,
Digguh, deedle,
Daidle man.

If I Were a Rich Man

(From *Fiddler on the Roof*)

When using CD, wait for 4 clicks.

Music by JERRY BOCK
Lyrics by SHELDON HARNICK

* Chord symbols are for teachers who may want to play along on piano or guitar to fill in harmonies.

**Boomwhackers®
Visual**

If I Were a Rich Man

(From *Fiddler on the Roof*)

Music by JERRY BOCK
Lyrics by SHELDON HARNICK

Melody

Copy for each student or use as an overhead transparency.
Color in the noteheads to match the tubes.

Let the Sunshine In

Tubes required:

(Tubes are listed in order of occurrence in the music for each part. For the "Low" tubes, use bass tubes or tubes with Octavator™ caps. Suggested tube distribution appears in the teaching suggestions below.)

Accompaniment Patterns:

Pattern 1 (and Intro and Ending): Low A   Low C   Low D   Low E   Low G♯
(Low G♮ replaces G♯ in the Intro and Ending. G♯ may be omitted altogether.)
Pattern 2:   Low G♯   Low E   Low F♯   Low B   Low A
Pattern 3:   Low F   Low G   Low A   C   Low E (tremolo)

Melody 1:   E   G   D   C
Melody 2:   C   Low B   Low A

Teaching suggestions:

MELODIES

- Listen to the full performance CD a few times, snapping on beats 2 and 4; then use the Boomwhackers® Melodies Visual (see page 49) to sing along.
- Consider just singing the melody (top staff on music score). Or if you have a unison or two-part choir, invite them sing this song while the other music students play the Boomwhackers® accompaniment patterns.
- If you decide to teach the melody on the tubes, teach by rote or use the Melodies Visual, color-coding the notes to match the tubes.
- Distribute tubes for Melody 1:
      One student holds E and G
      One student holds D and C
- Distribute tubes for Melody 2:
      One student holds C and Low B
      One student holds one or two Low A tubes
- Teach each of the two melodies separately before putting them together.

ACCOMPANIMENT

- Teach the three accompaniment patterns. Pattern 2 requires chromatic tubes. The G♯ in Pattern 1 may be omitted. The Intro and Ending is the same as Pattern 1 except that the G is natural. Each pattern is a TWO-MEASURE pattern.
- Distribute tubes for Pattern 1:
      One student holds Low A
      One student holds Low C and Low D
      One student holds Low E and Low G♯
- Distribute tubes for Pattern 2:
      One student holds Low G♯ and Low B
      One student holds Low E and Low F♯
      One student holds one or two Low A tubes
- Distribute tubes for Pattern 3:
      One student holds Low F and Low G
      One student holds Low A and C
      One student holds one or two Low E tubes (to tremolo)

- Teach by following the Boomwhackers® Accompaniment Visual Transparency (see page 52) that shows the patterns and their order.

ENDING

- Teach the Ending, which is really just the first measure of Pattern 1 with an A on the downbeat of the last measure and G♮ instead of G♯.
- Combine the melody with the accompaniment.
- Play along with the CD accompaniment Track 18.

EXTENSIONS

- Add a rainstick and the "Yeah!" at the end.
- Have some students display their tubes in a "V" peace sign if desired.

Let the Sunshine In

(From *Hair*)

Music by GALT MacDERMOT
Words by JAMES RADO and GEROME RAGNI

Copy for each student or use as an overhead transparency.
Color in the noteheads to match the tubes.

Melody 1

Melody 2 (down a third)

Melodies 1 and 2 combine starting in measure 15.

* See ideas for tremolo techniques in General Teaching Suggestions, page 2.

Let the Sunshine In

(From *Hair*)

Music by GALT MacDERMOT
Words by JAMES RADO and GEROME RAGNI

When using CD, wait for 4 clicks.

* Chord symbols are for teachers who may want to play along on piano or guitar to fill in harmonies.
** See ideas for tremolo techniques in General Teaching Suggestions, page 2.

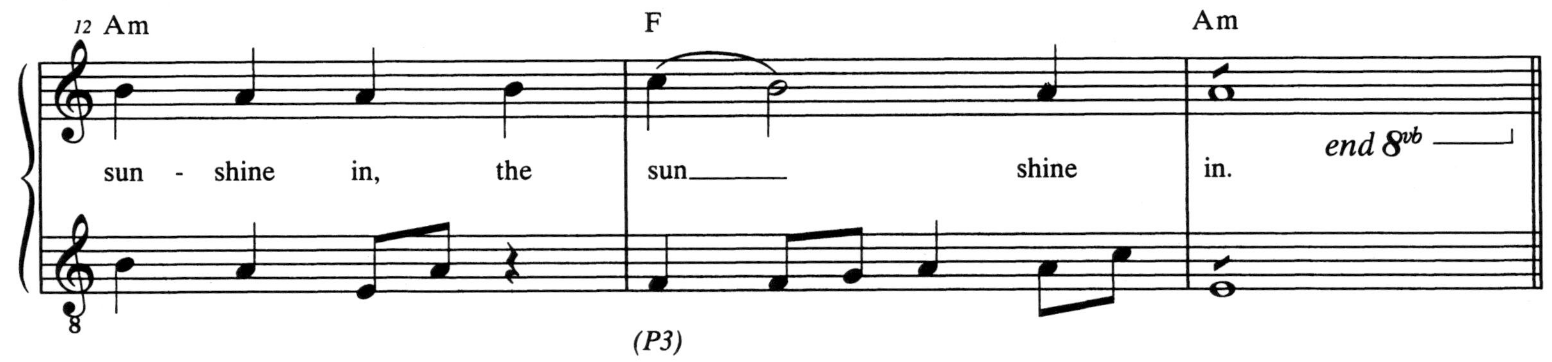

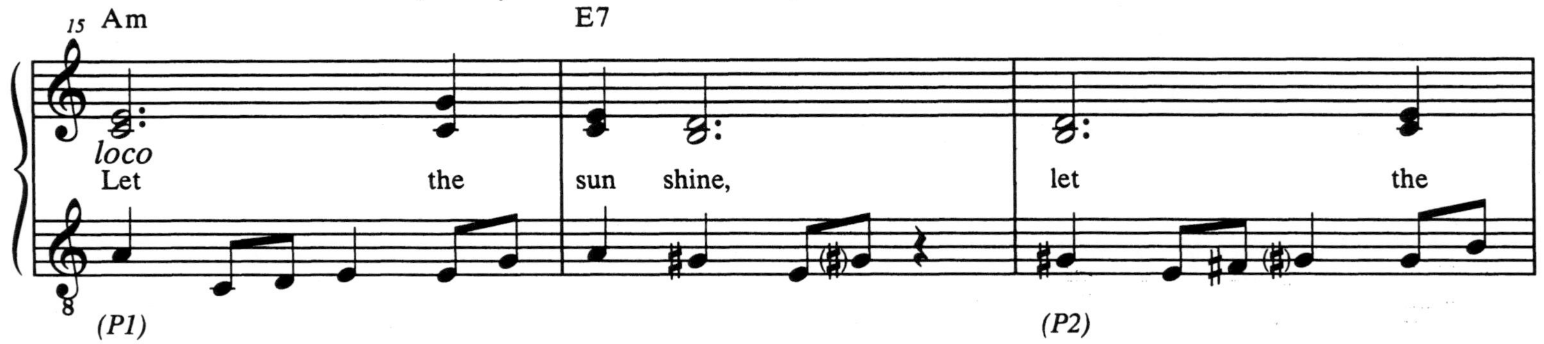

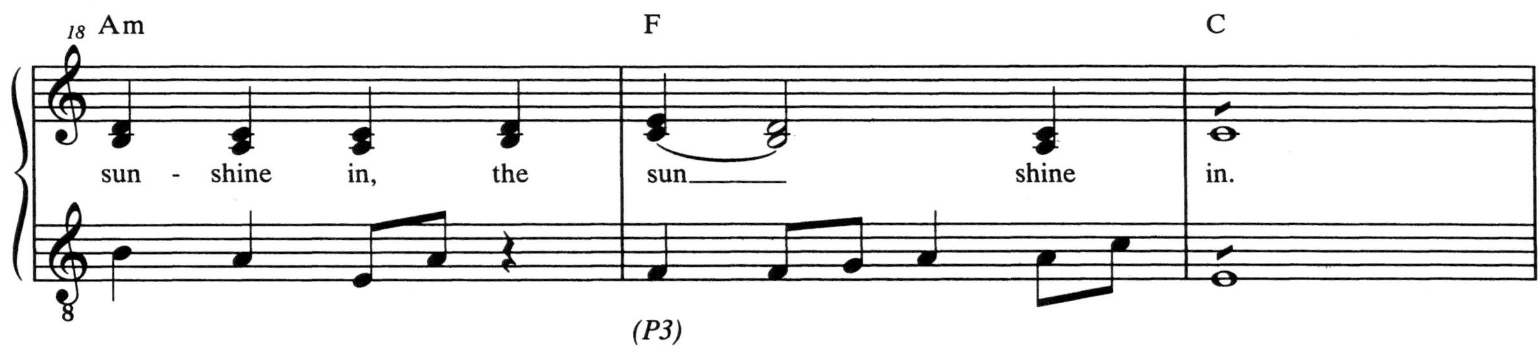

* Display Boomwhackers® in peace sign if desired.

Boomwhackers® Visual Transparency

Let the Sunshine In

(From *Hair*)

Music by GALT MacDERMOT
Words by JAMES RADO and GEROME RAGNI

Accompaniment

Copy for each student or use as an overhead transparency.
Color in the noteheads to match the tubes.

* Display Boomwhackers® in peace sign if desired.

One Boy (Girl)

Tubes required:

(Tubes are listed in order of occurrence in the music for each part. For the "Low" tubes, use bass tubes or tubes with Octavator™ caps. Suggested tube distribution appears in the teaching suggestions below. Notes in parentheses in the music are optional notes.)

Melody: It is suggested that the melody be used from the CD or played on a keyboard instrument.

Chorus

Pattern 1 (and Intro):	Low C	Low G	Low E	Low B
Pattern 2:	Low D	Low A	Low G	(very optional: Low F Low E)
Pattern 3:	Low F	Low A	Low D	
Pattern 4:	Low D	Low A	Low G	Low B (opt. tremolo: measures 34 & 36 on Low F, Low G)
Pattern 5:	Low C	Low G	Low E	Low A

Bridge

Pattern A:	Low F	Low A	
Pattern B:	Low C	Low E	
Pattern C:	Low C	Low A	D
Pattern D:	Low G		

Ending: C   G   High C (tremolo)

(This song will require five diatonic sets and 25 Octavator™ caps, without doubling any parts.)

Teaching suggestions (accompaniment only):

- Listen to the full performance CD a few times, snapping on beats 2 and 4; then use the Lyric Sheet Visual (see page 60) to sing along.
- There are five patterns for the chorus section and four patterns for the bridge. The melody is played on the CD, but you or a student could play it on a keyboard instrument. You may choose to omit the bridge. If so, you can jump from measure 20 to the final chorus in measure 29, omitting the eight-measure bridge. Or you could just have students sing and not play on the bridge, which works nicely with the CD accompaniment track. (The bridge is not hard but requires learning additional patterns.)
- Demonstrate swing eighth notes and straight eighth notes by clapping. Show the difference in the music notation:

Play the CD again, and ask students if the eighth notes are played straight or swing-style at the beginning (swing-style). Have everyone practice pat-pat-clap-clap-pat-pat-clap-clap as swing-style eighth notes while listening to the CD.

CHORUS

- Teach the chorus section by rote or by using the Boomwhackers® Visual (see page 58) and color-coding the notes.
- Distribute tubes for Pattern 1 (and Intro):
    One student holds Low C and Low G
    One student holds Low E and Low B

- Distribute tubes for Pattern 2:
    One student holds Low D and Low A
    One student holds Low G
    (Low F and Low E are very optional.)
- Distribute tubes for Pattern 3:
    One student holds Low F and Low A
    One student holds Low D and Low F
- Distribute tubes for Pattern 4:
    One student holds Low D and Low A
    One student holds Low G and Low B
- Distribute tubes for Pattern 5:
    One student holds Low C and Low G
    One student holds Low E and Low A
- The descending notes at the end of Pattern 2 are optional. Pattern 1 occurs more often than other patterns; assign parts accordingly.

The order for the chorus patterns including the intro, which repeats:

P1	**P2**	**P1**	**P2**	**P1**	**P2**	**P1**	**P3**	**P5**	**P4**	**P1**
(Echo in measure 12)	**P1**	**P2**	**P1**	**P3**	**P5**	**P4**	**P1 (no Low B)**			
Low C on downbeat of measure 18										

- The Soli (echo) in measure 12 answers the melody. Practice this part separately. Have the Pattern 4 players plus the Low E player from Pattern 1 play this part.

BRIDGE

- If you choose to teach the bridge, teach Patterns A–D by rote (or by using the Boomwhackers® Visual and color-coding the notes).
- Distribute tubes for Pattern A:
    One student holds Low F and Low A
    (Or player of Pattern 3 could also play this part.)
- Distribute tubes for Pattern B:
    One student holds Low C and Low E
- Distribute tubes for Pattern C:
    One student holds Low C and Low A
    One student holds two D tubes
- Distribute tubes for Pattern D:
    One student holds Low G, which could be played by the student who is playing Pattern 2.
- Have other students look at their Lyric Sheet (see page 60) and sing along softly while the Bridge Pattern players practice their part.

Bridge Pattern Order:

PA	**PB**	**PA**	**PB**	**PA**	**PB**	**PC**	**PD**

- The final chorus starts just like the first chorus, but the patterns are slightly different to lead to the ending:

P1	**P2**	**P1**	**P3**	**P5**	**P4**	**P5**	**P4**	**P1**	**Ending (final measure)**

- Practice the tremolos in measures 34 and 36 if you choose to do them. See the General Teaching Suggestions on page 2 for tremolo techniques. You may play just the standard Chorus Pattern 4 throughout these two measures.
- Practice the final measure, having the Bridge Pattern players play this part:
    One (or two) student(s) hold(s) C and G
    Two students hold High C (to tremolo)

One Boy (Girl)

(From *Bye, Bye Birdie*)

When using CD, wait for 4 clicks.

Music by CHARLES STROUSE
Words by LEE ADAMS

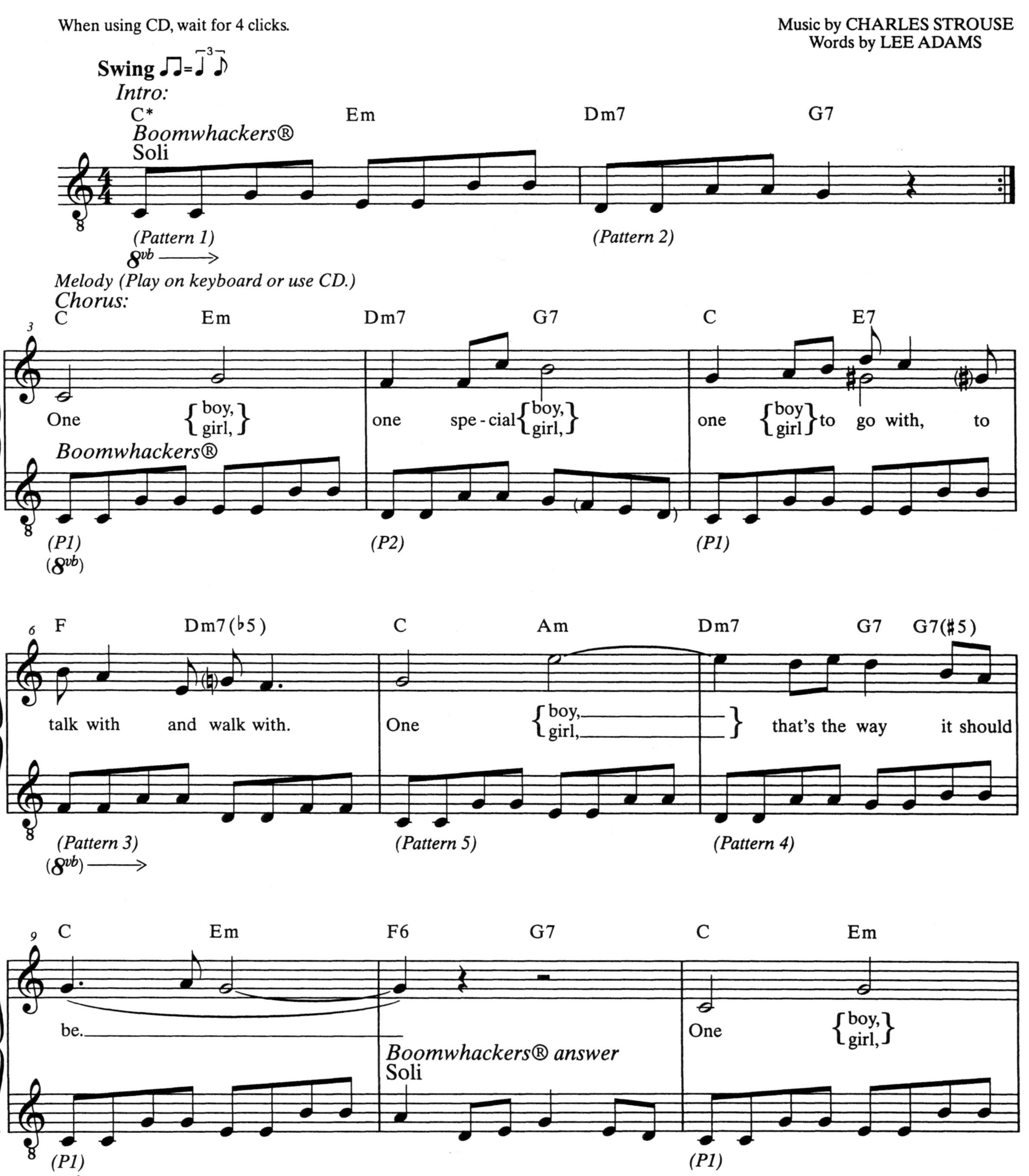

* Chord symbols are for teachers who may want to play along on piano or guitar to fill in harmonies.

One Boy (Girl) - 3 - 1

12 Dm7   G7   C   E7   F   D7(♭5)
one   cer - tain {boy, girl,}   one {boy girl} to laugh with,   to   joke with,   have coke with.
(P2)   (P1)   (P3)
(8vb) ———>

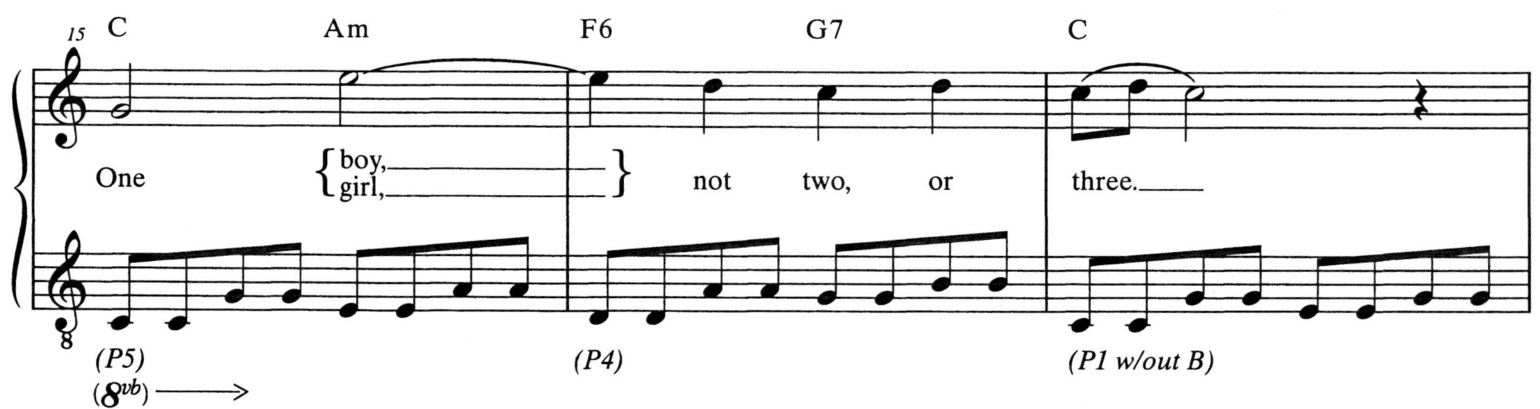
15 C   Am   F6   G7   C
One   {boy, girl,}   not   two,   or   three.___
(P5)   (P4)   (P1 w/out B)
(8vb) ———>

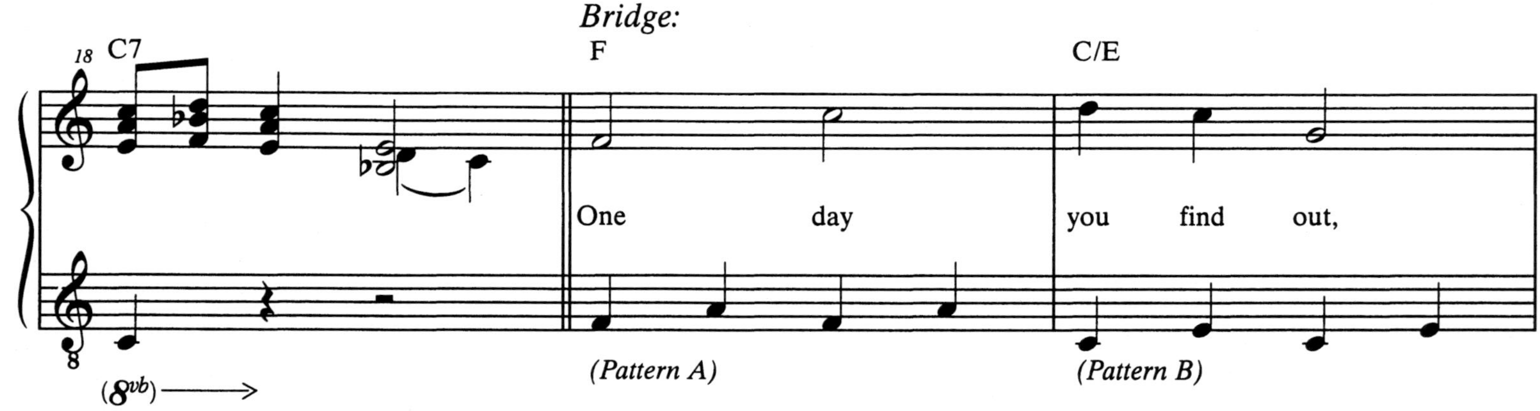
Bridge:
18 C7   F   C/E
One   day   you   find   out,
(Pattern A)   (Pattern B)
(8vb) ———>

21 F   C/E   F   C/E
this is what life is   all a - bout.   You   need   some - one who
(PA)   (PB)   (PA)   (PB)
(8vb) ———>

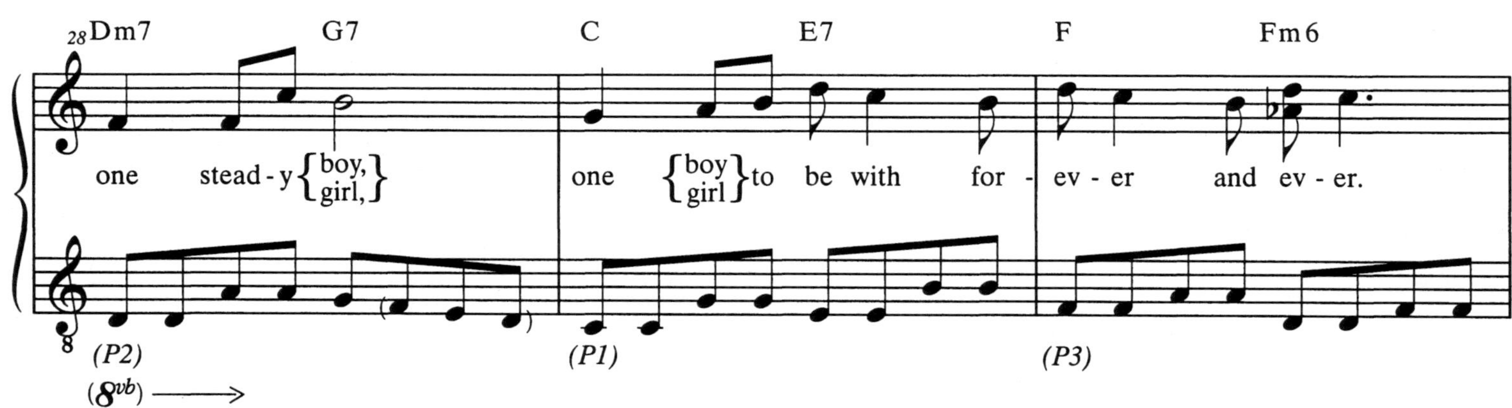

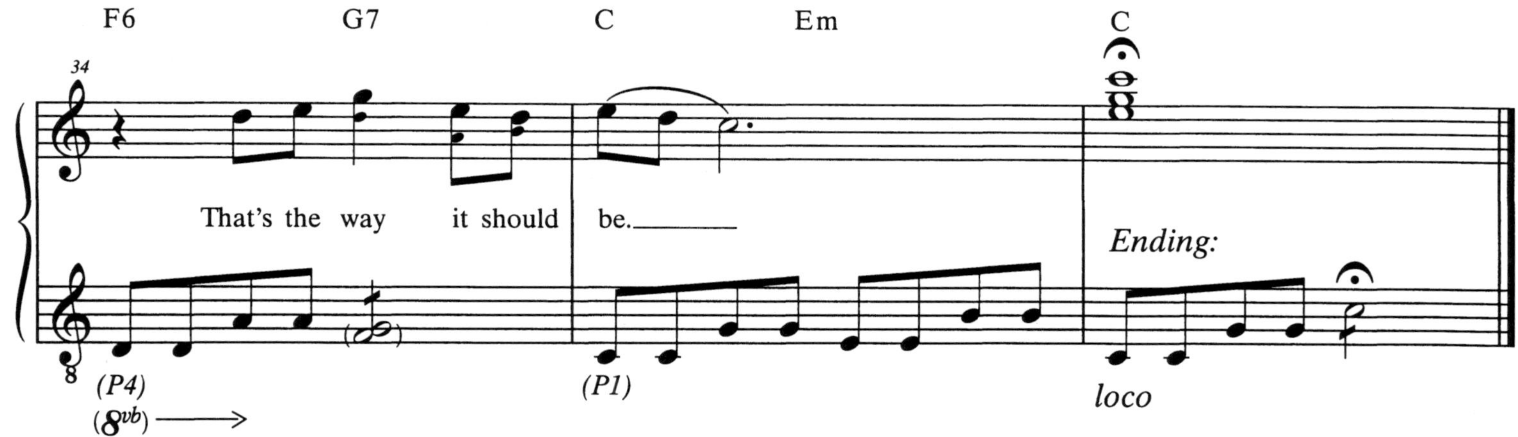

* See ideas for tremolo techniques in General Teaching Suggestions, page 2.

**Boomwhackers®
Visual**

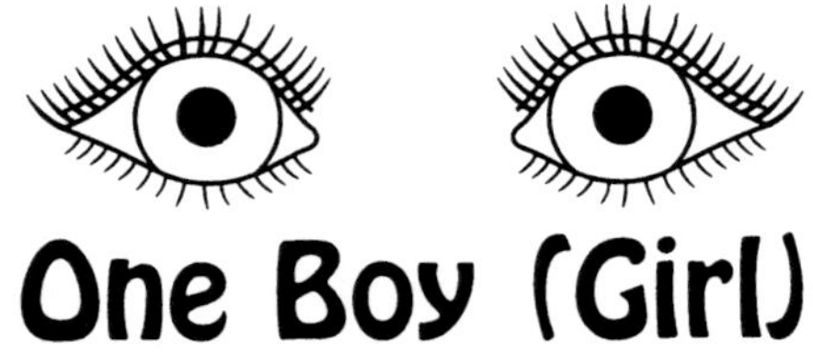

One Boy (Girl)

(From *Bye, Bye Birdie*)

Music by CHARLES STROUSE
Words by LEE ADAMS

Copy for each student or use as an overhead transparency.
Color in the noteheads to match the tubes.

One Boy (Girl) - 2 - 1

* See ideas for tremolo techniques in General Teaching Suggestions, page 2.

Visual

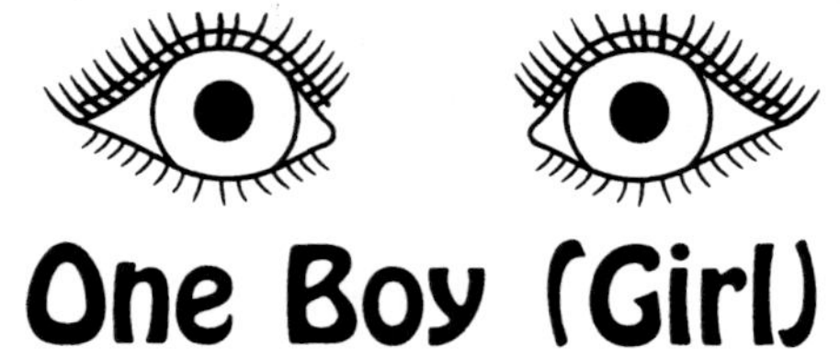

One Boy (Girl)

(From *Bye, Bye Birdie*)

Music by CHARLES STROUSE
Words by LEE ADAMS

Verse:
One boy*, one special boy,
One boy to go with,
To talk with and walk with.
One boy, that's the way it should be.
One boy, one certain boy,
One boy to laugh with,
To joke with, have coke with.
One boy, not two, or three.

Bridge:
One day you find out,
This is what life is all about.
You need someone who is living just for you.

Chorus:
One boy, one steady boy,
One boy to be with forever and ever.
One boy, that's the way it should be.
That's the way it should be.

* "Girl" may be substituted for "boy" throughout the lyrics.

Teacher Notes